This Book Is Dedicated
To:
Aunt Millie

Table Of Contents:

At Home:

You turn the
water on,
and it takes 20
minutes for the
water to get hot
or even warm

You have an uncle that knows everything, and we call him the "Answer Man"

Every time you go to the bathroom, there is a wasp on the blinds and no one knows where they are coming from

You go to
shower and the
water is brown

The phone
keeps ringing
all hours of the
night, and it is
a fax

Briefcase gets stolen in front of your house, out of your car, while someone is watching

Someone backs their car into your car when your car is parked in the driveway

The whole class
is about
Viagra, and it
is an advanced
business course

Big tree falls
on your house,
after you got it
accessed that it
will not fall

Go to open the door and the door comes off the hinges (not muscle man)

Random people
walk in your
garage and look
around

Busses park their busses so you cannot get in your driveway

Brother and his
friends
make noise, and
you cannot study

Cleaning lady brings friend, friend clips us for lots of items

Your aunt slips and falls down the stairs, and we have no idea how she fell

Aunt walks and takes food from the neighbors' gardens

Dog pisses on
your lawn
while you watch

Try to be nice
to your aunt's
father-in-law,
and you get the
4th degree
black belt

Someone shoots
a rocket into the
siding of your
house

Your lawn is a
garbage center

Someone takes
your lawn
chair from your
driveway

Someone steals your power cord that you need for charging

You cannot build
something in
your own
backyard

Get into trouble for taking care of your lawn

Go to get water, none left, like a bus of people came and drank all of it

Get soaked by
the
sprinklers

Garage door opens when it feels like it

Front door eats
the key

Cat/dog won't let you out of your own house (guarding the front door)

Cannot play ball
outside because
in the middle of
the day, the baby
is sleeping

At Work:

Can't get in the
building to work

Phone won't
stop ringing

Everyone is sick
for two weeks,
you have to do
all the work

There is no more coffee, & there's no coffee shop in sight

Copy machine
makes
random copies

Set up the copier to collate & staple, staples every page & collates backwards

Computer does whatever it wants

Get made fun of
because of age

Have to do all the leg work because of my age

Have to catch
a cricket before
the boss comes
back
(try finding one)

Go to mop
the floor & a
kid kicks the
canister & all the
water falls out

Go to get the garbage & everything falls out

Someone put a cherry bomb in the bathroom, only man, have to clean it

Get locked in the fridge

A pile of crates
fall down on you

Not allowed to make coffee after 3PM

It is pouring rain,one of the workers breaks into your locker and takes your umbrella

Have to run after
a burglar & get
into trouble
for leaving post

Card everyone under 40, she looked under 40, carded her, she screamed & made a scene

Get into trouble for helping a customer

Not going fast
enough

They don't want
you to get fired,
but they want
you to quit

We don't have
this product,
yes we do

Ink explodes all over your clothes

No pens in the
entire office

UPS leaves
package outside
a busy street
and it gets
stolen, you get
blamed and you
were off that day

Work as a team,
end up doing all
the work

Say it's casual Monday, have a memo that's says it, come to work no casual Monday

Ceiling decides
to come down

Told you misled them when you told them you have no idea about the product, get into big trouble

At School:

No security
when you need it

Professor thrown
up against the
glass, gets cut

Can't use the computers, security issue (not a computer issue)

Not one parking space

Get your
hubcaps stolen

Can't learn
until the door is
opened

Professor has
food coming,
can't teach until
it arrives

The whole class is about Viagra, and it is a advanced business course

Only 3 students in the class so we only get to learn for 30 minutes of a 3 hour class

Professor speaks broken English

Get a bath when
the professor
talks

Can't sneeze
in the class, if
you sneeze, he
screams

Locks the door
3 minutes before
the class starts,
and you cannot
come in

Talks on the cell phone for the whole class

Never shows
up, sent his
daughter to give
us homework
while he waited
in the car

Never comes
for the final
presentation,
can't present

Only tells jokes,
learn nothing

Gives you a term paper the last week of class

Makes you purchase a $300 book and never uses it

Knows nothing
about the subject
they are teaching

Professor throws your work in the garbage

Professor calls
you names,
makes fun
of you, and
screams at you

Correct a professor, and you get an F even though you had evidence supporting your argument

Get accused of prostitution and pimping for posting "sell your stuff" (example of a book)

Go to dinner for one of the classes

Have a partner
that lives on the
other side of the
world, never up
when you're up

Mixes you up
with another
student & gives
you their grade

Get stuck with a
partner that does
not want to work
ever

Have a teacher that picks on you every class for the whole class

Get beat up and
get kicked out
for hitting back

At The Doctor's Office:

You have the
first appointment
& there are
four people
ahead of you

You wait 2 hours
to see the doctor
for 5 minutes

You wait 2 hours to see the doctor & the nurse comes out only to tell you to come back next week

You go see
the doctor &
he thinks your
someone else

You go see the doctor after he ordered an x-ray & he says we should have that x-rayed

You get a call to come see the doctor (from the doctor), rush over, and asked why are you hear?

Go to one doctor, says one thing, go to another doctor in the same office, says the complete opposite

You get a prescription, go to fill it, can't, not your name on the prescription (typed not written)

Go to the doctor
for a bad cough,
next week have
a rash

Waiting in the waiting room, person next to you pukes on you

Waiting in the waiting room, person next to you squirts blood in your eye

The doctor takes your insurance, nope not any more, have to pay full price for visit

Have to blow your nose in an ENT office, just finished getting probed, no tissues, can't leave the chair (they ran out)

Go to the doctor for help, doctor won't help, too scared

Go to the doctor, never reads the chart, asks the same questions every visit, does nothing

You are told
you have an
appointment,
nope sorry

You get your
blood taken,
you get a call
you have --------
later they tell
you the lab
mislabeled your
blood

You go see this doctor, it's at her home, you see her children running past you

You go to the doctor's house, she has a candy dish, you take one and chip your tooth, thecandy was from 1998, it's 2011

You go to the
doctor and she
puts the moves
on you

The doctor tells you to jump off the bridge as a way to solve all your problems

You are in the
waiting room,
and this person
keeps taking
pictures of you,
you find out later
she posted them
online and not
good results

The doctor's office shredded your file and then blames you because you told them to

You go to the doctor, and he does not speak English

The doctor's office card says it is in one city, but in reality it is in another

You request this one doctor to do the surgery, find out later he left for the day, and the other doctor makes a mistake during the procedure

You go for a
vitamin shot, and
end up getting a
adrenaline shot

The doctor is so
rough, she cuts
you and when
she try's to fix it,
hurts you even
more

The doctor says "oh you are fine, nothing is wrong," you go to another doctor for something else, and they say why was this not checked

You go to the doctor's office and in order to get out, you have to have exact change, there is no change machine, no way to get change, your car gets towed

At The Hospital:

You come out of recovery, puking your brains & the nurse only cares about putting your information into the computer

They have no
clue what's
wrong & there
is clearly
something wrong

You are ready
to go home, the
candy striper
is taking you
to your car, he
goes over a
rock, you fall on
the floor

You need to give blood, it's her first time, she misses 10 times, you're in pain

You soil yourself,
you need a
new robe, only
allowed one robe

You are
bleeding, blood
is squirting
everywhere,
nurse says don't
worry, you will
be fine

You are allergic
to this medicine,
you tell the
nurse, she says
you are taking
the medicine,
you get sicker

The only thing
you can eat is
toast, you cannot
get toast

The alarm is going off, the nurse comes hoping she will help, she puts the silence on, because the noise is giving her a headache

You are ready to
be discharged,
but there are no
doctors in the
building so you
have to wait 3
days to go home

You slip in the tub, no nurse can help you because your nurse is on break

The nurse orders
your shirt off for
no reason at all

The nurse puts
your clothes in
the closet until
it's time to go
home, you are
ready to go
home, no clothes

The person
next to you is
screaming on
the top of his
lungs willy, willy,
willy all night
long

The person next
to you keeps
tapping you all
through the night

The person next
to you shits on
the floor every
couple of hours

The person complains about you because you have law & order on, and they don't like law and order, they demand to switch rooms

There are bugs
everywhere in
the room

The nurse's beard gets caught in-between the wires, and you are stuck to the nurse

You are all ready to go into surgery, you are put to sleep, an emergency happens, and they leave you there

You are being
transported
in the elevator,
the elevator
stops

You do not need paddles, but the doctor charges them and wants to use them on you even though you don't need them

You get a doctor in training and he/she is having a lesson while you're being treated

A cat jumps on the hospital bed with you in it

A person is calling for help in the bed next to you, no answer, you call the nurse in, she comes in and yells at you for calling her for him

The nurse falls
asleep in the
chair next to you

The patient's friend eats your lunch while you are going for a test, you can't get food until dinner

You get up to go
to the bathroom
and the bed
collapses

The bathroom door is locked in your room and no one has the key

They will not
give you your
medicine and
you get sicker

At A Restaurant:

You order chicken soup & you get ½ piece of a plate inside

You order cherry coke & get a regular coke with a cherry

You make a
reservation &
they give it to
someone cuter

The place is
empty & it takes
2 hours to get
your food

You get hit in the
head with a full
tray of food &
they blame you

You sit down on the chair & fall back

You order one thing, they give you another, & fight with you

You ask for thin food, get thick, call the manager, food is even thicker

The menu says one price, the bill says another

You give a 15% tip even when the service sucks, the waiter comes after you

You're sitting down eating in a fancy Italian restaurant & see bugs crawling on the wall

You call the manger over, says it is part of the atmosphere

You're sitting down eating in a fancy restaurant & it starts to rain inside

You're sitting down and eating in a fancy restaurant; the manager turns the fan on & you get covered in dust

You're sitting down and eating in a restaurant and a guest turns the light off you turn it on (goes on all night)

You tell them
you are allergic
to an ingredient,
told it could be
made without it,
order it, eat it,
ambulance

There is stuff
floating in the
water, you
question it, and
the waiter spits
in the water

You get a dirty
spoon, the
waiter cleans it
with his apron
and hands it
back to you

They use the
same cloth
to clean the
table as they use
to clean the floor

The food comes out cold, you ask them to warm it up and never get your food back

You ask for more bread, they say they don't have anymore, you see this new couple who just walked in getting bread

A restaurant with no menus, you can order anything you want, but you can't have this and that

As you are
eating the
lights grow
dimmer and
dimmer

You are eating in
the twilight zone,
random lights
flash periodically

They fire the best waitress and hire the worst

You go there for this particular item, everyone that goes there gets it, they stop making it because no one is ordering it

You ask for no anchovies, they say there are no anchovies, you are eating the salad and guess what, anchovies

You are a vegetarian, you ask for a veggie burger, you get a hamburger and the waiter does not even care

You order slowly
so that there is
not a mix up, you
are told to order
all at once so I
don't have to go
back and forth

You get the
check and
you have not
even gotten
a menu, and
the manager is
insisting you ate

You sit down, order, 40 minutes later you are told the kitchen is closed, never get your food

At The
Supermarket:

Store has only one cashier in the middle of the day on a Sunday

No milk/eggs

Bottle return is broken, no one wants to come

Can't move in
the store

Shelf says one price, rings up another

Have a whole
shelf of a
product & they
don't sell it

Person cannot
give change

Person will
not take a
manufacturer's
coupon that
does not expire,
but insists it did

Person will not take someone with 13 items in a 12 item line

Bread aisle is closed off

Get into a fight over a box of clusters with an old lady, she wins

Slip and fall

No bathroom for customers/only walk-ins

Go to return something to the store at another location, they don't sell that, can't refund money

Walkout of the store and get in the middle of a fight

The doors close on you and you fall down and get hurt, manager says be more careful

No carts to be found

No bags to be found

Nothing in the entire store is left but a can of pork & beans

No Lights,
Can't See

Cashier does not know how to use the register

Bag person fills
the bags and
they all break

Gives you the wrong change and cannot reopen the register

Someone backs their car right into you, you see it, and they take off

A child rams a
shopping
cart right into
your car

A person parks
in a spot next
to you and you
cannot get your
car out

Pigeons will not move no matter what you do

Kids rollerblading
and rams into
your car

Driving school is teaching someone how to drive on a Sunday in the parking lot, car stops every 2 seconds

Rings up an item
4 times and you
only have one,
refuses to take
it off

At The Movies:

You go to the movies & all the doors are locked in the middle of the day (people are inside)

You go to the movies, and order popcorn, they just had a bus load of people & they cleaned them out

You go to the movies & it's sold out

You go to the
movies & have
to stand for the
entire movie

You get gum on
your shoe

You go to sit
down, end
up on the floor,
get all wet

You sit down, an old lady with a feather hat sits in front of you, cannot see the movie (she will not take it off)

The kid in front
of you keeps
hitting you with
popcorn

You are asked
to leave for no
reason

The lady in back
of you hits you in
the head

The person in
back of you,
keeps kicking
the chair

You have to move because you are in "muscle man's" seat

The sign says one movie, you end up watching something else

You buy milkduds, & the box is empty

You are kissing a
girl & 3 people
come with a
wand & flash
you continuously

You buy one
ticket & get
another

The person next
to you is talking
& talking

A person is talking on the cell phone for the whole movie

The lights stay
on so you
have a glare

There is no
sound

All the
bathrooms are
closed

Ask for one
ticket, get two &
no refund

Car gets towed
in the movie
theater parking
lot & you go see
a movie

There is no ac, walk out soaking wet

Slip on the sweat from others

You bring a jacket, someone else takes it & says it is theirs

The person next
to you puts their
hands in your
popcorn and
eats it

You find a
receipt on the
bottom of the
popcorn box

You get locked in the bathroom

Forget your ticket with your friend, have to buy another one (went to the bathroom)

At A Theme Park:

Get on a ride,
only one that
runs out of gas

Get stuck upside down for over an hour

Get stuck in an inside ride with no lights and animal movies

Aunt hits her head on the seat because the ride makes you go back

Get cotton candy,
and everyone
eats it, you get
nothing

Get cotton candy
and all the bugs
in the whole
park attack it

Buy a ticket but cannot use it

Candy apple
is rotten, will
not refund your
money back

Coffee is bitter, vendor says you're lying, our coffee is never bitter

It's all about
the money,
more money no
waiting in line

Park closes in 2 hours, pay same price for an all day pass

Go on a ride,
scrape your
entire leg

Go on the slide
and get stuck on
the top

You clearly win something, and the person will not give you the prize

Win something,
take your
picture, come
back with your
friend, friend
cannot claim
prize because
you won

Crane picks up
the item, get so
close, drops

Water gun game,
tie (have to split
the prize)

Get soaking wet
on the bumper
cars

Ride gets stuck
on the top
and rocks

Wire comes
down and almost
fries you

A 4 year old is
too big to go on
a kiddy ride

Same theme park, different rides take different tickets

20 tickets to go
on one ride

Wait 3 hours to
go on the ride,
you are next,
ride is closed

Go on a ride, exit puts you on the other side of the park, takes over an hour to get back where your parents are

Go on the only
ride with no seat
belt, no one tells
you, ride starts,
you know the
rest

Go on the merry go round, and instead of going around you go up and down

Ride cannot be
turned off

Give a crying child a prize you won, get hit by the mom

40,000 tickets
gets you
nothing but junk

At The Repair Shop:

Oil change takes
30 minutes tops,
waited over
3 hours only car
in the shop

I can fix it, nope

Car gets broken into, behind locked doors

You get accused
of stealing their
magazines

They don't know
what's wrong

You slip on oil in
the waiting room

You go for an oil change & leave, the door comes off when you go to get out of the car

You go to fill the wiper fluid & air comes out from the other side of the car

They fix
something &
heavy damage
happens
because of them

As soon as you drive away, all the oil comes out of the car

You have a
pool of water
in the front &
passenger seats

They look at it, say it is going to cost x you say no & they charge you for telling you how much it is going to cost to fix

They damage
your car in the
shop

They get into an accident with your car

They put the wrong inspection sticker on (got it for x and put last years on)

They borrowed
your cds, never
gave them back

They put a
broken radio in

They burnt wires in your car, so it does not run anymore

Put the wrong tires on

Never balanced the tires on the car

Take your light bulbs, and don't give them back

Go in for an oil change, come out with needing 10 other things

Never do the oil change, but you pay for it

Never put the bolts back on the tires

Get your air conditioner fixed, now stuff from outside blows in your face

Windshield wiper
went flying off
the car after
getting it
replaced

New battery lasts 4 days

Have to tow your car so you can take it home, and charge you because they had no room

Give you the
wrong keys and
make you pay
for new keys to
be made

Brakes only last
2 weeks, did
more damage

At The Airport:

They think your
Indian when you
are Italian

You ask a stewardess for help & she says she is not on duty

You get your hair pulled by an old lady

You sit next to
a women with
claustrophobia

A baby throws
up on you

You get your
bag taken away
for no reason
(really) she
wanted my bag

The stewardess
opens the
soda and it
goes all over you

You get pushed
out of the way

Your foot gets
run over by the
beverage cart

A child drops his oatmeal on your head

A kid squirts you with his water gun

Gum is thrown at you

A man kept
puking right
next to you

A lady sleeps on your lap and will not wake up

You get your
pillow stolen
because
it is more
comfortable
then the one the
airline provides

You buy one
ticket & get
another

You have the same printed ticket as someone else

They lose your
luggage in
the overhead
compartment

The person
next to you just
randomly takes
your drink and
drinks it

Below zero air
blows in your
face, cannot turn
it off

You get locked in the bathroom

You   go to flush
the toilet & come
out blue

Three people
have to wand
you, not just one

This is not your driver's license,but you look like the person in it

Someone puts
your shoes
on and keeps
walking

The pilot left the plane

The beverage cart scrapes the skin off your leg

Had to pay for bottled water

Changed the gate, told no one, all the passengers were waiting, plane leaves

Got hit on really badly

At A Hotel/Motel:

You tell the front desk you are going to be late to check in, they say no problem, you get there late and the front desk is closed

You have a non-smoking room and it smells like you are in the room of a chain smoker

You go to a famous resort, and there are bugs in the bed

You go to a famous resort and when you turn the water on, bugs come out with the water

You go to a
famous resort
and a college kid
comes through
your wall

You are sound
asleep, all of
a sudden the
window blows off

You go to the same motel for 15 years, the door never locks so you leave the key in to go get a towel that is drying. You get locked out and there is no way to get back in

You find a bug in your bed, the "manager" says they are friendly bugs, and they come with the room

Continental breakfast is until 11AM, you get there at 10AM and the "concierge" will not put out any more food

You are starving,
it's 7AM, the
breakfast place
just opened
a "swarm" of
people come
(a family) and
eat everything
before you can
walk up to the
food

You ask for scrambled eggs you get poached, when you ask why, I never scramble eggs

You put the "Do Not Disturb" sign up because you want to take a shower, and the maid walks in on you

You are told this
is a quiet place,
and from 9PM to
4PM there is
loud noise, and
banging on the
walls

Whenever you
flush the
toilet, the sink
leaks and
you get wet

It's not a water bed, but you get wet and no one knows why

You are not
allowed to close
the windows
even when water
is coming into
the room

You are swimming in the pool and someone randomly comes in who does not belong to the hotel, and starts swimming and talking to your 5 year old cousin

They charge you
a fire drill fee

You come out
to find your car
vandalized, and
the manager will
not do anything

You have to
pay extra to get
clean towels

The hotel shut
off the hot water
so you have
to take a cold
shower

There are no
lights in the
room but just
one little lamp

The TV only
allows you one
channel, and it's
not in English

Children are playing catch, you ask them to stop, the ball breaks your car window

You check-in, go out to dinner, come back, someone else is in your room

You bring
4 pairs of
undergarments
and put them
in the drawer,
only find 2 in the
drawer the next
day

The air conditioner goes on, goes off, they replace it and that one is worse then the other (spits out water randomly)

You put your suitcase on the ledge, the ledge falls down, you now have the suitcase and the ledge on top of you (the suitcase was empty) had to pay $300 for repair

You go in the shower and slip, break the glass, get all cut up, have to pay $500 for repair

Grandma screams, you break the desk, break the lamp, have a permanent scar and a reminder of a very bad day):

Bonus:

You really like a girl, she really likes you, you are too shy to do anything

You like this girl
a lot, she likes
  you, she calls
you, you hit your
  head running
with joy up the
  stairs, start to
    bleed

You meet this
girl, she comes
dressed in a
costume in the
middle of August

You take this girl to the train, she leaves her nail clippings in your car, they have dirt all over them, she bites them off

Sitting at dinner, she pukes, you have to change (all over your face)